Dan Michael

THE SEASONS OF OUR MINDS

THE SEASONS OF OUR MINDS

Poems by

IAN MICHAELS

EXPOSITION PRESS   **NEW YORK**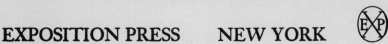

for lillian, christopher,
diane, tricia, sarah, and c.

Cover design by Ian Michaels

First Printing, April, 1972
Second Printing, November, 1974

EXPOSITION PRESS, INC.

900 South Oyster Bay Rd., Hicksville, N.Y. 11801

FIRST EDITION

SBN 0-682-47489-4

contents

chapter one
the winter of my mind

chapter two

where are the flowers, where is the sun

chapter three
springs love, peace, beauty, and warmth

chapter four

silent colours of autumn

the seasons of our minds

to everything there is a season
and a time for every purpose under the heaven

chapter one

the winter of my mind

the winter of my mind

i trace your smile
in the winter of my mind
your ruffled hair
undone as the autumn trees
as i feel for the wings of love
the majestic meadows of your beauty
stand still in this endless moment of time
as you sleep transfixed
in the winter of my mind

october 25

i wrote a poem
with the vision of your company
and kissed you with poetic rhyme
a flood of thought that never stops
in these endless hours of time

october 30

with autumn's breeze behind me
i held you with my lips
telling you how much i care
with soft caressing fingertips

as summer leaves fell to autumn's ground
you were standing up on your toes
our lips were speaking in silent sound
in the only language we know

while autumn put the summer trees to sleep
we held summer's peace in our minds
and tomorrow's wine where our lips did meet
if only the whole world could find

october 31

putting your dreams in your hands
reach up high to the heavens
to scrawl them on the sky
and give forth light to the day

for nothing within is out of reach
of those sought dear to us
to share in the foward days of tomorrow

november 4

i got your note the other day
you told me that your parents were religious
and that i shouldn't be afraid

tomorrow falls in different ways
for those that don't look back
but reach up high for the fruit it brings

won't you reach up with me

november 5

as autumn leaves fell to cobble stone
you wept along silent shores
through memories of your mind
while my thoughts told me
that we need the worthy affection
of a warm friend in more than just words

we have something so new
yet so old in tradition
as it lies in a maze of thoughts
and in your hand which is hidden in mine

with quiet clouds above
you touch me with a smile
and in words of silent teardrops
that fall to greet a friend . . . me

november 7

love is the child of freedom
where seasons change direction
it sits looking at rainbow coloured clouds
and says
   i'll catch the wind
      if you ask me

coloured in skies of prussian blue
and in words of silent teardrops
it's written in poems and laughter
often shared by two
falling upon mirrored reflections of life
tasting each precious moment
before it passes by
and says
   i'll catch the wind
      if you ask me

november 10

the night is tatooed with stars
through clear skies showing
its astronomical beauty
in nighttime thoughts
that are tatooed with your stars
of heaven's caressing fragrance

forgive me for not knowing
your astronomical beauty
as i know the stars

16

my silent loving touch
will change that though
by morning's hour

november 10

to touch your love again
i'll paint you in radiant colours
in spring's spirit of youthful pleasure
in summer's rose of nature's beauty
and in winter's snow white purity

you will be my canvas
and i will be the paintbrush
with my hands guiding your vision
as i take you to tomorrow's gallery

november 12

do you know any effete snobs?
some of them wear buttons
that say what they are
while others wear mickey mouse watches
that tell time in executive offices

i man the battlefront
protecting your body
from the sounds and words of hate
we don't need someone to teach us hate
we need someone to teach us how to love
and live in peace, is that wrong?

november 13

we didn't speak with words
the silence filled the space
our lips were all we heard
as we lay there face to face

november 14

love is like a bird flying blind
as it floats through soft translucent air currents
you go wherever the currents take you
as you smell and feel the experience of living
feeling beyond the nowness of today
to the paradise of tomorrow

november 17

you are me
and i am you
as we lie here
the two of us
cast in each other's image

you see me for what i am
and smile
as i see you for what you are
telling your lips with mine
i love you

18

november 18

do you know how beautiful you are?
and that if you look into my eyes
you'll see what beauty really means
because my mirrors never lie

november 20

i was late once
when you waited for me
on your favorite bench
where you called me
all sorts of things
that you don't call friends

it's funny how quickly
you forgot those things
when your eyes met mine
and my lips met yours
and we tasted love's wine

a time when birds are leaving
a time when summer clouds go to sleep
a time for sun tan people dreaming
a time for autumn trees to weep

a time to walk through coloured leaves
a time of seasons' changing hands
a time to look for winter's peace
the time our love began

november 22

i'm only but a man
so try to understand
the thought of a beauty yet unseen
the thoughts that call out to be free
where in the corner of my mind
there are words not meant to be blind
these feelings that i must face
not in dreams but in life's embrace
to share you through tender tears
to hold you in tomorrow's years
to share the presence of your womb
and whisper the words that i love you

let me guide you
through the gates of life
where i'll comfort you
as my hand reaches out
and gives you
the security of tomorrow
as we lay exposed
to morning's hour
and i
glancing at your pure white form
stroke your rose cheeks
in love's warmth
as my smile reaches
beneath your tears
before it gently senses
the truth between our lips
in poetic rhymes that say
i love you today and always
as i'll guide you
through the gates of life

on november nights in the park
i sat by the river where there is a tree
where i carved names
when i was younger
and from where i watched
day melt into night

there were people then
walking their solitary ways
as the autumn breeze caressed them
in its unhurried flight
people going places, doing things
all oblivious to the sounds of the city

those were pleasant times i think to myself
as i sit by the river where there is a tree
where i carved names when i was younger

i watch and i watch and i watch
for there are no more people
on november nights in the park

november 29

my thoughts surround you
as the sounds of your breath
mix with the music of love in the air
love's sentiments will not crumble here

for there are no cracks or holes in our walls
our walls are built with our trust and love
and love's best virtue is seen in trust
therein lies life's radiance

december 1

i woke up in dawn's morning
with you on my mind
your fragrance like a rose
was all around me
mixing with the early morning dew
as the sun came through clouds

i thought that your presence
would compliment this winter's day
from dawn's morning hour
rising on a soft balloon afternoon
that floats to meet the evening
and our presence together
lost in the folds of evening's blanket

december 2

the night breathes with heaven's stars
as we look out of picture frame windows
where the moon shines on curtain lace
leaving filigree patterned shadows

now that's a beautiful sight to behold
and i have one better than that
for yours is a beauty beyond compare
beyond the night or the "rubáiyát"

omar khayyam knew the richness of beauty
he wrote of it in life and love
but if he could ever have beheld you
his persian classic would not have been enough

december 4

let the day turn gently over with us
into evening's warmth
each intensifying the other
the evening with its snow white pearls
you with love's perfume like a rose
and i with an angel in my arms
in a day of evening's warm

the time when our eyes first did meet
and love passed within our reach
made words of silence an ultimate feat
for to see in love was better than speech

your eyes spoke first, making mine more rich
to see love call out its name
to see this pleasurable sensation which
meant more to me than fortune or fame

in time we knew more than just our names
our vision often filled with happiness tears
for now we were playing adult-like games
using silence that no one could hear

we're brought to silence quite often you know
in feeling that words are not enough to express
our unified thoughts as our love does grow
between our eyes, our hands, our lips, and our breasts

so in days whenever we touch to meet
with love passing within our reach
we make words of silence an ultimate feat
for to feel in love is better than speech

december 9

as the morning awoke
pools of gold sunshine
swept through the curtains
of filigree and lace
to the snow whiteness
of your soft skin
that brought me
unspeakable pleasure
in yesterday's midnight hour

i kissed you without asking
with just an intimate knowledge
of your lips, your body's warmth
as we became one with the day
with pools of gold sunshine
reflected in our love

december 10

my arms wrap around you
like a birthday present
one gives forever
for i have given you laughter
    when tears would fall
i have given you warmth
    in winter's halls
i've brought you comfort
    on lonely nights
i've written you poetry
    to read in love's light
i've given you wisdom
    when we were free
and more than this
    i've given you me

december 11

in a nighttime of white lace
we held each other's reflections
and spoke fragments of our thoughts
through lips that touched again

you were not wearing cosmetics
only your inner self which i prefer
as my hands caressed your unmade face
with the makeup of our love

december 12

you asked me how i felt about abortions
the reason things are like they are
is because of the church
it's okay to tell your followers what to do
but not people of other faiths

imagine what would happen
if the rabbis prohibited pork in restaurants
the other religions would cry bloody murder

i think we've forgotten how to be human
with abortions illegal, and wars legal
with penalties for crime less than smoking
i feel like a rainstorm
behind clouds that want to cry

december 14

i see many things with my eyes
i have seen you in sunlight
under prussian blue skies
and i have seen you in evening's hour
covered by a blanket of stars

yet the most important time to see
is not with the eyes, but with the lips
when i tell you in unspoken words
              i love you
that is the most important time to see
when my lips feel your presence
and your lips see me

december 15

in days of joe namath
you were worried

there's a difference you know
your brother is addicted
to football and television
while i'm addicted too
but to soft radiant hair
that lays undone in my hands
to sweet cherry lips
that melt on mine
to soft snow white skin
that smiles on me on translucent nights

we're not like television shows
our show never ends

december 18

until the dawn wakes in the sky
my body turns and so do i
to see your face so gently warm
to hold your love already born
your aesthetic smile my lips can see
in that which is longer than a memory
to taste your sweetness in heaven's air
to see our love played everywhere
to make us warm when weather's cold
the time we spend, you turn to gold
painting my smile with the beauty of your grace
again to touch your lips, your face
these times we share will always grow
my dearest love, i love you so

30

december 19

today you touched me
and this man was a child
as our thoughts twined together
in the darkness of love's shadow
where no one.could see
how lovely and beautiful we were

but there is tomorrow
and then another day
when i shall ponder the emptiness
that separates us in time
till monday morning rises
and we are together again

december 22

i awoke this morning
to find the sun bleeding upon us
you were in silent sunbeams
as i lay listening
to the morning breathing
the very air that we shared between us

i glanced at your sleeping form
as gentle as a tender dawn
kissing you as my lips led me
to the valley of your bosom
where you found me
with love dancing in your eyes
your perfume touching my senses
and the sun bleeding upon us

december 25

couples in the park are laughing
you can hear the laughter
as it comes through the wind
holding hands they walk their way
happiness has come today
for those, they're not alone

food vendors they sing their song
whistling as they walk along
on a bright winter's day
snow white flakes that make the floor
glistening in the sun's splendour
silence has come again

i walk the lonely roads i take
thinking as i contemplate
that space by my side
i hear the music of the wind
telling me i cannot win
your touch in days gone by

as petals of my heart fall down
who am i, a lonely clown
on grounds i sometimes know
strolling lovers keep their way
happiness has come today
for those, they're not alone

december 27

the days between us are far and wide
to be overturned like autumn leaves
in states unbound and loosely tied
in patterns too long to read

to try to read unwritten verse
the hours of the day
i'd rather quench an empty thirst
there is no easy way

time can quickly deceive the sight
but not put out the fire
our words will reach beyond this plight
for love knows not to tire

december 28

i'm like an incomplete puzzle
like most of us
looking for that something
or someone
that will make us whole

there are no stores
that sell these missing pieces
because they can't be bought
with money
although some may say otherwise

you might be able to find it
in a gentle smile
in understanding eyes
or in soft warm hands
that hold the passing seasons

i'm only what i am
but i'm incomplete without you

december 31

a place called childhood
lost like a tree in winter
you stood there and cried
stones of blue
           gleaming in your eyes
tears of fond memories
falling over cheeks
of mirrored roses
scattering cherry blossoms
           on the ground
love's wine that improves with age
to be remembered
in dreams you see
but cannot touch
           in a place called childhood

the purity of the morning's dawn awakes
as i set myself on a homer's journey
this odyssey takes me over unmanned regions
of a beautiful paradise

the sun draws venus shaped shadows on me
as i pass through love's forest garden
where the flowers of heaven's rich gems
bloom in aphrodisiac fragrance

the garden ends
where a soft snow white human beach begins
under which i can feel tremors
in a pulsating beat of life

i'm drawn into a valley
surrounded by a lustre of warmth
that continues up a steep embankment
where the love on my lips was touched by yours

to hear the word love is a beautiful thing
to see love . . . is heaven's odyssey

january 1

i watched the sun chase us
from morning and your sleeping presence
through afternoons of strolls in parks
to evenings of unending pleasures

as we awoke in the newborn light of today
with the morning before our eyes
and the sun holding its mask around us
you asked me what we'd do today

let's watch the sun chase us

january 3

i waited
by your windowsill at sunset
for you were not there
as i stood by myself
thinking of times
when we were happy
wondering of times gone by
thoughts that take me
to darkened corners of my mind

i remember when happiness
fell upon our love
when we walked in parks
filled with children's laughter

now i stand
in silent shadows of the night

as winter's breeze
sweeps through my hair
freezing tears
like glass threads of crystal
listening to the sounds of the evening
keeping company with myself

when it's time
i'll get up and leave
leaving my dreams behind
until then i'll wait
wait by your windowsill at sunset

january 4

i follow traces of the wind
to touch your love again in the air
the winter wind that carries autumn leaves
and floats them like soft balloons
caresses me from the train station
and takes me past houses that i recall
where i have walked in times before
i followed traces of the wind

january 6

in the union of time
and time again
the wind warps me
as winter bleeds upon me

i dare not mark
where i have been
for the trail is over
as i lapse back to tomorrow
through mile on mile
of newly awakened dawn
turning in shadowy places
of no colour, of no time
i am undone
       as the autumn trees
               in winter's snow

january 8

it snowed last night in the garden
winter's child swirling in ophelia white
scattering the heavens over the ground
and orphan-like branches
an incredible silent whiteness
always laughing remotely
as its long white scarves of winter
covered all in its reach

soon its winter breath ceased
under the night covered with pearls
and as fair as a cameo

and as innocent as a new born babe
the child went to sleep
last night . . . in the garden

january 9

will you help me look for spring
in the shadow of winter's snow
where we took summer strolls
barren fields where flowers once lay
silence where children once played
i walk where winter's branches
are made heavy by the snow
where we sat among growing flowers
in pebbles and unraveled leaves
the white wilderness is lonely
in a silence beyond words
will you help me look for spring

if people would only try hard enough
we might have peace
like the peace and love
that we share between us

only at evening's time
when the dark is all around us
do we play war games
as i conquer boundaries
unmanned by other foes

in morning's daylight hour
you surrender to me again
before making my coffee
which i sip as i read yesterday's
                war casualties
if people would only try hard enough
we might have peace

january 14

you kissed me before spring came
making my winter sunny and bright
you changed the wings of birds to glass
as they glistened through winter's sunlight

you made silent sleeping flowers bloom
by just holding them in your soft warm hands
you made my poet's pen make love with you
as we walked along the white winter sands

you turned me into winter winds
in night winds that caressed your perfume
as i glanced at your seasonal smile that said
winter winds play to love's spring time tune

january 19

if i had wings
with them i would fly
to paradise rainbows
beneath star blue skies
i would be able
some time and some place
to look at the stars
to find your soft face
more heavenly bodies
do not exist there
'tween sunshine and moonbeams
your soft silken hair
deep in your eyes
blue crystal like tears
falling like jewels
through heavenly stairs
i'm there by your side
where angels do sing
these times how I wish
i only had wings

january 21

my destiny within me
no longer empty dreams
for you have filled the emptiness
with happiness it seems

a flower within me
that blooms in clear blue skies
you have let the sun come out
of clouds to make me wise

my soul stands forgotten
it's naked to the wind
there are some things you cannot do
to someone who has sinned

a light shines above me
to be seen by the blind
for God's the only one to give me
strength and peace of mind

january 26

you are my flower of happiness
my bread and my wine
as my eyes are pierced
with your beauty
my lips lingering on yours
my hands softly touching
your graceful contours
the softness of your skin
love's fragrance like a rose
growing all around me
like a flower of happiness

january 28

beauty is an entity of unlimited time
as timeless as the oldest wine
a limitless expression of one's own thought
something expressed or something sought
the kindly words from a friend
that seem to never ever end
it's balloons of pastel coloured clouds
children's laughing summer sounds
from breaths of spring to butterflies
or little children asking why
where cherry blossoms fall like rain
where nature sings along the plain
it's a couple walking along the shore
in silent colours across the floor
it's people washed by summer sun

a time when lovers become one
a time when wars and killing cease
a time when all we know is peace

and that's what beauty means to me
a time for all humanity

january 29

i passed the hilton hotel the other day
and thought
wouldn't it be nice if i lived there
so i went into the lobby
and made believe i was a guest

i bought one of the paintings on the wall
the one that you liked so much
then i asked the elevator man
if you came yet, but you didn't
so i said hello to a neighbor
before i stepped out
where a taxi was waiting
to take me to my next daydream

february 5

the naked walls envelop me
the windowpane's above
the dawn remains in window shades
and deposits sun above
and i amid the barren walls
there are other ways to see
to see the silence of the day
as it envelops me

february 6

it's so easy to fall in love
yet so hard to break away
your presence gave me happiness
in my lonely hours
the sun came out of yesterdays
in bright yellow smiles
you read my poems
and thought me all sorts of things
you read my mind as i read yours
and you became afraid
afraid of being hurt again
is it so wrong to be involved

so on this quiet winter's day
as i lay on my bed
my hands searching the emptiness
that was once you
while my eyes look at the floor
for your shoes which aren't there
it's so easy to fall in love
yet so hard to break away

february 8

my mind was wandering
with the wind as my shadow
as i walked over winter paths
that were traveled by few
surrounded by the flowers of the night
as they shone in a night close to sleep

you once transformed the paths i walked
to soft billowy white clouds that moved with us
but now they were as still as the night
and my mind was wandering
with the evening as my shadow

february 13

i reach out and touch
the empty whiteness beside me
feeling the warmth
that you brought me in yesterdays
in pervading darkness
my thoughts ache
with hollow loneliness
as night surrounds me
telling me that i should be asleep
instead of reaching out
for the empty whiteness beside me
the loneliness of tomorrow

february 15

my winter sun grows colder here
since hearing your renouncement of me
better if from your lips i did hear
the words that only your parents could see

if their extremes you also share
my love and poet's words not enough
better to end then in doubtless care
although my heart still carries love

visions will fade as the morning's mist
mortal minutes take time in days
my flame will go before it is missed
and i'll continue in life's endless maze

march 1

spring is just around the corner
a happy time for couples
and walks through parks of poetry
but i'm in no rush
because you won't be there

sometimes i feel
the sight of coloured kites
and rainbow skies
children's laughter
balloon men's cries
might end my endless winter
but i don't think so
because spring is just around the corner
and you won't be there

48

march 3

when the skies are darkened
God puts out a hand to me
will i be tomorrow
wait and see, wait and see

there are words of wisdom
staying in some people's dreams
except if you're a kennedy
or a martin luther king

they have seen the mountain
and they have seen the falling rain
they have seen the suffering
the misery and the pain

while people looked for what should be hidden
and not that waiting to be found
our potential goes undiscovered
in words of silent sound

while my sisters and my brothers
are looking to find a better day
only when we hold all our hands
will we strive to find the way

and so as skies get darker
and God puts out a hand to me
will we be tomorrow
wait and see, wait and see

chapter two

where are the flowers, where is the sun

for the record

are we masters of the wind
i really don't think so
for it's been a long time
since peter, paul, and mary
and the answers are still
blowing in the wind

a dream

i had a dream last night a while
a ray of hope was seen
i saw people hold hands, i saw them smile
but why in just a dream

i dreamt of seeing birds fly high
with a message for all of mankind
white doves of peace flew in the sky
to peace man's sometimes blind

i dreamt of seeing black and white
some yellow and some red
holding hands in heaven's light
they'd rather live instead

i dreamt of seeing flowers
i even saw the sun
under rainbow coloured showers
bringing peace where there was none

i had a dream last night a while
a ray of hope was seen
i saw people hold hands, i saw them smile
but why in just a dream

may 6, part one

one day there were voices, of peace they did sing
alive with the wind in the breath of spring
one day there were sandra, allison, jeff, and bill
now there is silence, those four they are still

four of many to keep the dark from the sky
in questions they asked, for peace they asked why
a war that was far, is it now near
in those shots that were heard is there reason to fear

some go to pray and some march for peace
the cause those four had will not die or cease
they died for a purpose, for peace not in vain
for people need peace like flowers need rain

may 7, part two

red is the colour of a stripe
near another that is coloured white
like the stars that are on the blue
like the thoughtless men that numbered few

for red was the colour on the ground
and white was a prayer falling down
while blue was the colour of the sky
turning grey because it wanted to cry

for beneath the flag of the free
death danced in the land of liberty
four people who spoke of peace, not of hate
were silenced "my god" in an american state

the judgement

they sit waiting
with thoughts of fear
bleeding on their foreheads
while an eternal prayer
presses deeply on their lips

for their son
the brightness of their yesterdays
is absent in their presence
fighting . . . for who knows why
he exists in letters
written with trembling hands
that have been taught to kill

hands that once held
a favorite wooden sailboat
that he took to the pond
sunday afternoons after church
the house of the Lord
where he was taught
to love thy neighbor
and how in the Commandments
and under Matthew 5:21
it says "thou shalt not kill"

now they go and pray
that they are not among those
who are told every week
that their brightness . . .
their pride and joy
has been darkened

but who commands the judgement
and who commands their son

a flower grew

over hills where flowers grew
where sunbeams play in morning's dew
where trees are bathed in morning's light
a soldier rests wounded in fight

the sweat in beads lies on his brow
glistening in the sun that shines there now
where was the sun the day before
when he was in man's game called war

somehow it's different from what they said
enchanced it's not, it's hell instead
his skin is pale under clear blue skies
where heaven takes the hate from his young eyes

his body is still, it does not quiver
as he lies beside the flowing river
where flowers once grew in morning's light
where a life has gone from wounds in fight

find a rainbow

once a baby, once a boy
playing with his favorite toy
taught to love and not to hate
hate will soon decide his fate

find a rainbow, find a dove
find a flower, find your love
where the days are shining bright
you'll find a peace in heaven's light

once a baby, now a man
gone off to a foreign land
taught to love and now to kill
fighting on a crimson hill

find a rainbow, find a dove
find a flower, find your love
where the days are shining bright
you'll find a peace in heaven's light

some men lived and some men died
some men laughed and some men cried
but still they teach to hate and kill
except to those on crimson hill

words of darkness

words of war are like iron
that rust in people's minds
they wither growing flowers
and thoughts which soon run blind

they put out burning lamps
flanked only by our brain
which sees not in the dark
nor the cries of falling rain

where are the flowers, where is the sun

carbon monoxide fills the air
sulphur dioxide everywhere
flowers that grow and bloom in may
silence as they quickly fade away

where can they run, where can they go
in shadows that tell them they cannot grow
where are the flowers and where is the sun
where are the smiles from everyone

near 100 men were killed this week
in a government's war that reasons weak
the president calls it a gradual withdrawal
those caskets that return are dead one and all

why have they died these men who braved
their lives for dictators so far away

is it to find the flowers, the sun
where are the smiles from everyone

four students were killed at kent state
they died in an atmosphere of hate
some people felt that they deserved what they got
are these the ones that fired the shot

war and hate and polluted clouds
will the voice of reason call out loud
where are the flowers and where is the sun
where are the smiles from everyone

chapter three

spring's love, peace, beauty, and warmth

sixty-eight

spring is just over the horizon
bringing days of baseball, parks, and flowers
in tulips, daisies, and daffodils in bloom
may's fingers that interweave with the breeze
as it floats over watery glens
pushing fleets of sailboats on their way
passing couples walking with lovelight in their eyes
and tomorrow held tightly in their holding hands
under springtime cotton candy clouds
that let rays of golden threads pass through
to children's smiles and laughter

spring's love sits just over the horizon

sixty-nine

the sounds of the season
are painted on the springtime air
as the sounds of reason
are painted on your presence fair

by nature's children like flowers
that grow beneath waves of sun
your cheeks of pink rose colour towers
over feelings shared by more than one

while the sun paints the aqua sky
on the sailboat waters below
a happiness shines within your eyes
where blue crystal visions know

those tears are shed for happiness
in being close to a new friend
the winter's gone and so is the loneliness
maybe the spring will never end

the sounds of the season of spring
bring tomorrow closer to today
for to see the colours that happiness brings
is to know of peace in a better way

seventy

is this love
i heard the wind say
as it saw my mind
on blue dreams of saturday
that held only your visions
while someone else held you

i've been held before
in the moon's yellow haze
with other soft visions
sharing them with others
and not bothered by it

but now it does bother me
that you're with someone else tonight
as the shades of darkness
stare at me in silence
only the wind cries out
in your absence

is this love?

seventy-one

i touched you and felt you tremble
beneath your garments
and beneath my fingertips
trembling in the sensations of love

in a world that only we shared
to touch with longing eyes
and to caress with parting lips
we touched and felt love tremble
as we gave birth to the beginning of spring

seventy-two

you held me tight
in rain and thunder
but there was no reason
to be afraid
for darkened streets
reflect light's shadow
as night turns into gold
and april showers
bring flowers to may
and to those who are afraid

warm is a time
when i take your sad words
and make them better

when i push grey clouds aside
to let the sun shine in

when there is no reason to be afraid
because i am near

when i carry your thoughts
gently on my mind

when flowers grow
through winter, spring, summer, and fall
where the seeds of love
are forever joined

warm is a time
a time for us

everybody is part of everything
part of heaven, part of hell
part of winter, part of spring
silent thoughts where people dwell

how much more the sun
that shines on prophet-like walls
can man also shine as one
standing short or standing tall

as the day is part of the sun
and the stars are part of the night
people are united as one
under God's eternal light

like falling april showers
that fall on rich green plains
that bring forth may-type flowers
calling forth your gentle name

because everybody's part of everything
and as we stand up as two
like flowers need the spring
you are me, and i am you

when i hold you
a flame in my heart
wants to reach out
and bring you into me
into an emptiness
that is no more

when i hold you
your skin speaks
with an infinite warmth
as soft as a summer's breeze
that surrounds me like an island
in the month of may

when i hold you
it's as if i hold
the flowers of life
beneath my bosom
hoping that dawn never comes
to wake the moment's time

seventy-six

my heart it sees with one eye only
its name, they call it love
and when it sleeps in night it's lonely
for dreams are not enough

seventy-seven

i cannot say goodnight my love
because it is not so
for if these words were meant to be
we'd not part evening's glow

for as this hour passes by
two hearts held in a dream
if they could touch, if they could know
what goodnight really means

a goodnight is when two never part
and when time never flies
it's when two people hold hands tight
from night till morning skies

and so until the time comes by
when we can hold hands tight
and wait in sleep till morning skies
i cannot say goodnight

seventy-eight

standing by the reflections
of the morning as it wakes
as the sun breathes through trees
where we'll stroll through future dates

listening to the minutes
as they pass on morning's breeze
dew drops like crystal
from beneath green coloured leaves

watching as the day blends
yellow sunshine through your hair
as the sun smiles all around us
breathing love's warmth everywhere

feeling through our senses
as the day sings out her tune
in brightly coloured flowers
that caress us in perfume

holding in our hearts
the love and peace that these things bring
as we stand by the reflections
of the days of early spring

seventy-nine

in a mood of softness
my eyes turned the morning over
to find you snuggled in dawn's blanket
lost in a world of dreams

your hair was hanging loosely
revealing paths my hands had left in a night
that echoed the birth of our breaths together

it's nice to see you look that way
before you wake up
and we glance at each other with tired smiles
giving with each other's endowments
in a mood of softness

eighty

you met me at the door
where i held you in my arms
my lips meeting yours
and your feet silently leaving the floor

before inviting me in for dinner
you said, first let's drink the wine while it's cold
it was good, but the dinner was better

later your eyes smiled at me
as i asked you
to turn the day gently over with me
but first let's drink the wine while it's cold
it was good, but the night was better

eighty-one

we'll rest on a bed of roses
as their fragrance fills the air
with love and springtime laughter
as the sun shines soft on your hair

i'll caress your beauty and grace
my hand on your warm gentle breast
where you'll feel intensified pleasure
as we rest on our soft springtime nest

my eyes speak softly to yours
as our mouths fuse slowly into one
we'll lie with our hearts both together
till sleep gently closes the sun

eighty-two

in fragrant gardens of spring
we rolled over green blades of grass
gathering the morning dew
in our sun glistened hair

being stoned
on our own energy
getting resonance from the sun
and from each other's presence
is more inviting than
drug's artificial boundaries
that knows not the tears
of true happiness

the happiness which lends itself
to the togetherness of love

eighty-three

i surprised your mood of softness
with a sudden rush of passion in my limbs
as we listened to spring and tchaikovsky
with the midnight air surrounding us

you were too sleepy to remember
the dancing of my finger's touch
or the wind that turned us into night
before my lips said goodnight

when i saw you the next day
you could only remember the undone paths
that my hands had left over you
maybe soon you'll remember the traveler
and i . . . those paths by heart

mornings of sunny side ups
with light creamed coffee
and warm sleepy kisses

they only number a few now
but maybe with the help of summer strolls
and white glistening decembers
will the numbers become endless

endless like the poems i write
each one saying i love you
in a different form
while you need only do it one way

in mornings of sunny side ups
with light creamed coffee
and warm sleepy kisses

the silence among spring and flowers
like the silence of unspoken words
a language of eternal lovers
is seen far more than it's heard

it's feeling the distance between two
a sensitive tongue and tender lips
it's touching the beauty that's around you
in caresses of warm fingertips

it's smelling love's perfumed fragrance
and breathing the air that you share
through all of the seasonal tints
it's being with one you hold dear

it's seeing one's enchanted smile
it's living a life meant for two
it's letting your eyes talk awhile
each seeing the words "i love you"

the sky is of the water's blue
the leaves are of a distant green
a stroll is of a sunday afternoon
love is, and so are we

a rose is of a ruby red
the seasons change like scenery
a word is something softly said
love is, and so are we

a star is of the evening's light
the day weaves through life's tapestry
your touch is something softly white
love is, and so are we

eighty-seven

my lips played love's melody on your bosom
breasts touched by my moistened kiss
grasping empty air before feeling
before sensing
before joining beauty's warmth
like the sun touching flowers
in sensations that bloom and grow
taking spring's tune
and making it better

eighty-eight

it takes time for frost to thaw from branches
and flowers to bloom in spring
but take my hand in comfort
and watch the happiness it brings

it takes time to reach decisions
especially in one's troubled times
but take my hand in comfort
and i'll make your cloudy days shine

i once had troubles and problems
i had them just like you
when someone gave me a hand in comfort
and a flower of happiness grew

so now when days seem colder
due to problems that they bring
just take my hand in comfort
and we'll see another spring

eighty-nine

if you need a friend
envisioned in warmth and understanding
and gently sensing truth in people's minds

let your eyes reach my smile
lean your head gently on me
and let your dreams flow through mine

for i am only but a friend

ninety

the week has only seven days
sometimes i wish it were more
so i could say i've seen you
those seven days and more

ninety-one

your soft reflection
was captured by silent sunbeams
as they fell to the cool
penetrating water's surface
where i tried to hold you
in my cupped hands
and bring you to my lips
where i could kiss
your soft reflection
and taste love's wine

ninety-two

i bought you some flowers
one yellow and one red
to put my thoughts in words for you
in colours softly said
please let us grow with you
if only for a while
for even if the days are few
they'll bring love's tender smile

ninety-three

you should watch my lips
when we lie down softly in the day
or when we lie down at night
because when you are all i see
and when you are all i feel
the words "i love you" will caress my lips
and reach out to touch yours

ninety-four

on a not yet summer's day
i sat and watched
as spring's breeze
played upon the water's edge

it danced on the white sand
swirling in silent sunbeams
around my shadow
looking for yours
to bring it warmth
on a not yet summer's day

ninety-five

red wine on my lips
or was it just a blush
neath crystal in your eyes
that softly drew my touch

a tongue's taste of honey
two eyes shut in haste
in minds quickly nourished
two beings in embrace

our souls ran together
like the sun with the day
two hearts beating softly
affections closely stay

our minds gently opened
to dancing fingertips
and to thoughts that we had
with the red wine of our lips

ninety-six

some rose coloured flowers and me
that's what was left
when you flew like a butterfly
to be gone seven days, a year

some rose coloured flowers
that brought happiness to a tear
and made nights shine like day

and i, who told you things
a mirror could not
in making your dreams become real
while my dreams now carry me
through elusive winds
that carry you so far away
but not your touch
which lingers still
on some rose coloured flowers
      . . . and me

ninety-seven

peace is within me
on this soft sunswept day
as it carries my thoughts
so far, far away
past rainbow balloons
and blueberry skies
past rose coloured flowers
where happiness lies
where spring sings a song
that floats on the air
to pink coloured lips
to one that is fair
where fragrant perfume
fills up the day
where my loved one blooms
on this summer's day

ninety-eight

with clouds gently flowing overhead
and the world seeming to go another way
i looked up to see a lonesome cloud
that lost its way, never knowing rain
that makes flowers grow in poetry
and people scatter in all directions

i wanted to write a poem on the sky
to comfort the cloud as i have you
when you have lost your way
in the silence of the day
so i collected my thoughts
and looked up again
but the cloud was gone
and the world seemed to be going another way

ninety-nine

i woke up at four a.m. this morning
and found your hand folded in mine
just as you had left it when the night was awake
when we lay in the boundaries of each other's shadow

you were outlined in the night's filigree of white moonbeams
with your hair gently blown on me
like the wings of a butterfly
fluttering in the breeze of a summer season

our hands were like a warm spring shower
that played with the minutes
giving life and energy to the flowers of our bodies

now the spring shower lies in sleep
in the seed of two hands held together
where flowers grow in love

one hundred

the evening will cover us
as it's a long time
from summer's night to day
but not long enough
to enjoy the fruit it brings

in the moon's intimate perfume
like stars that reach their zenith
we're lost in a galaxy of love
a heaven's silence that is deep
in a darkness that covers us
as we both fall asleep

one hundred and one

sometimes i want to reach up and touch the sky
on a lazy sunday afternoon stroll in the park
i could too, if you pushed some clouds away
but not today, i'm here alone
because every now and then
i like to walk by myself
understanding myself as well as others

i pass an oak and then a willow
my feet walking over traveled paths
fields of green grass growing all around
while my mind grows in thoughts with myself
and the wind breezes through newly born leaves

thoughts of yesterday, today, and tomorrow

tomorrow is just beyond the sun and your touch
and i'll be able to reach up and touch the sky again

your dreams awaken you're on your way
over golden fields where the sun does rise
the air surrounds you with morning dew
with swirling soft prussian blue skies
walk or run summer winds you'll play
as it flows through your radiant hair
the wind will kiss and caress your face
as you are so lovely and fair
you look around with bright gleaming eyes
green hills below you, blue skies above
you breeze through currents soft and warm
your smile tells the world you're in love
the sun will chase as you try to fly
with the birds as they glide through the air
your eyes look up at the cotton clouds
as they follow you everywhere
you smell the flowers' perfumed fragrance
as you pick some to put in your hair
you think of someone that's close to you
and the happiness brings you a tear
you stand up still as you look ahead
in rainbow coloured skies that look wild
the sun is leaving to sleep its head
as it leaves you, a summer love child

one hundred and three

i watched the roses today
as they were being blown in the wind

they reminded me of you
and your tousled hair
as we ran yesterday
through summer's breeze

i guess a rose is a rose

                    . . . is a rose

one hundred and four

we walked hand in hand
                with the rain
under skies reflecting
the grey concrete slabs of streets
looking at buildings
from years gone by
with their time-weathered porches
and paint that ages to the ground
in a solitude of grey clouds

i wonder when i'm time-weathered
if i will join their solitude
or be with you
walking hand in hand
                with the sun

one hundred and five

when the sun is gone
and the petals of a rose fall
when spring and summer
are covered by winter and fall
when your thoughts and tender lips
no longer mix with mine
then i'll know that i have passed
the happiness of time

one hundred and six

more beautiful than a rainbow's glow
more precious than a ruby rose
more saintly than the winter's snow
my love you're more than words will know

one hundred and seven

the rain whispers low
so as not to wake the flower
that sleeps under darkened skies

for there is a rare precious beauty
that lies hidden in the sleeping form
to be awakened only by the sun
while the flower sleeps in the knowledge
that the rain will not bend
and the sun will not weaken

i know . . .
for i am the rain and the sun
and you are that flower

one hundred and eight

where are the stars that shine at night
empty colours on evening's wall
that whisper in shades of loneliness
over sounds of your unanswered call

i was reading some poems and thought of you
to hear your voice but within this time
on the telephone i tried to get through
just to bring stars that shine to my mind

ringing, just ringing
not a voice of hello was there
ringing, just ringing
darkened corners and thoughts that were bare

i passed the time and it passed me
and the emptiness brought me a tear
as a smile soon turned to sorrow
for that voice of hello was not there

one hundred and nine

should i keep vigil over the dying night
while your presence is gone in touch
for now you are filled with sleep
like a cup that runs over the rim
while i am filled with memories of a living night
where we touched outside and in
and my mind was ripening with your touch
as i felt as wild as the wind

now i have lost you to the black darkness
that stops even the wind in blindness
a wind that tried to keep vigil over the night
and failed . . . in the absence of your touch

one hundred and ten

i don't know what our minds will say tomorrow
for today they speak of when our eyes first met
a memory i am fond of looking back at

some people may not believe what their eyes tell them
like children we learned to believe in ours
as we learn to believe in everything else
but there was more to us than what our eyes told
for our eyes were reinforced by what they saw
by our hands, our lips, our hearts, and our minds
that told us we were the sun on a newborn day

one hundred and eleven

passing highways outside my bus window
where traffic writes on monoxide walls
sleepy eyes that pierce the clouds
to let the sunshine breathe her calls

aging trees like willows crying
with clouds on all sides now
nature's tune and perfume dying
to let the sunshine in somehow

so many things people could have done
on their lost journey too
my god the day is dark, where is the sun
i'm on my way to you

the sun through carbon curtains seen
a path to reach your way
this bus it too kills fields of green
as it helps block out the day

i left the dark of traffic sleeping
packed up and went my way
where nature sings and life is still breathing
and sun puts on her day

i met you on a forgotten beach
where white is still a dove
where civilization cannot reach
the sunshine of our love

one hundred and twelve

my verse and love beside me lie
in dawn's endowments newly born
sleep has her near to glorify
from shades of evening to early morn

the sun awakes to nature's rhyme
to have her near to glorify
to kiss her lips of nature's wine
to take the sleep from her young eyes

awakened eyes that softly shine
to see love's vision and not a dream
to hear soft sounds of passing time
two lips, two hearts with love between

to have her near to glorify
my verse and love beside me lie

one hundred and thirteen

as we walk on the beach
the sun molds your image on the sand
as the tide reaches out to touch you
then ebbs back into the ocean
before reaching out again
to capture and treasure your presence
as i have many times before

but i am not a misty shore line
i need never let go

one hundred and fourteen

the day belonged to us
as we reached out
to caress the warmth of the day
while the sands caressed
            the warmth of our bodies
with the wind beneath your silken hair
your body gave way to the sun
with my hands around your bosom
your lips gave way to mine
            gently sensing our love
we'll catch tomorrow in our breaths
as the misty shore line tried to catch us
under faint winds of unwhispered rhyme
that told the sun's sand beach
            the day belonged to us

one hundred and fifteen

as the morning smiled in the sun's desire
you slept within my mind
as you lay there before me
under the gold complexion of the day
with the sun tangled in your hair
as it lay undone over my arm

we glanced at each other with mortal eyes
a lasting look, a long embrace
with eyes unbound in morning's light

like flowers that drink from the sun
i drank from your lips
and you from mine
as the morning smiled in the sun's desire

one hundred and sixteen

right near somebody's old beer can
that had been left in hours old
the sun painted your picture
on a canvas of golden beach snow
it used sunbeams to do your hair
in swirls of golden brown
and clouds to do your soft skin
in a pure white silent sound
your fragrance was like the sea breeze
as it quickly filled the air
to spread happiness to observers
who had seen your portrait there
right near somebody's old beer can
that had been left in hours old
where the sun painted your picture
on a canvas of golden beach snow

one hundred and seventeen

beyond the misty shore line
passing images of a love that's free
two people hold tomorrow
so that all the world can see

listening to the music of the shore
as it plays all around us
and the day breathing through our pores
as the sun softly fills us
with the divine creation of life
we become one with the universe

passing images of a love that's free
two people that hold tomorrow
so that all the world can see

one hundred and eighteen

the sun has given you new freckles
i can tell because i remember
the way your body was yesterday
when we were on the beach
listening to the waves
as the sun played on our bodies

my fingers passing slowly
over your warm summer skin
in soft silent strokes
remembering each freckle
as the moon does stars
so i could test myself
when the evening came
and the moon would kiss
our tired sun tanned bodies
and i, your new freckles

one hundred and nineteen

looking to find it in the night
in the depth of its darkened touch
i looked for the lights of stars
like the lights that i've seen in your eyes

lights of silent voices
that had beckoned me to your lips
that now lie fastened in sleep
in the slumber of the night

my eyes climb up beyond the skies
where in lusters they lie in wake
bleeding the sky in heaven's light
breathing across my face

i now have seen night's beauty
time held it shortly in your eyes
these grains of sand . . . of sleep
they have reached beyond my eyes

going wherever the summer winds blow
with a tin can at our feet
we stood beside the morning
on an unknown nameless street

standing with our thumbs out
watching people pass us by
human kindness in its presence
still we thought we'd give a try

then a caddy stopped to drive us
one with music in stereo
as they asked us where we're going
oh, wherever the summer winds blow

so we went by several beaches
under waves of yellow sun
where the water kissed the beach sand
and the people having fun

soon we got out by the wind flowers
yellow shades that seemed to flow
in love's rhythm that we too shared
going wherever the summer winds blow

the sun will soon devour the night
in the open eyes of the dawn
as we lie lost in no morning's time
and i just holding a yawn

the night stands not forgotten
though darkness did blind the eyes
our hands were touched in whispers
and the words became our eyes

eyes of radiance beneath the stars
and now beneath the sun
in these never ending moments
when the night and day are one

as i awaken to love's perfume
your form reaches into my eyes
asleep in assurance that i am near
brings your smile into morning skies
deep in sleep looking softly warm
a princess with sun-tangled hair
bouquets of flowers i ought to bring
to the girl who is sleeping there
my lips now take me your bosom's way
as the kiss will strengthen your snare
your hold on me is like the sun's on day
in soft words that no one can hear
open eyes gleaming down on me
softly touch my drowsy lit eyes
i look your way hoping that i see
your smile in the morning skies
sensual lips pressing onto mine
as my hands softly caress your form
the perfume of morning was all around
bringing love, peace, beauty, and warm

chapter four

silent colours of autumn

photographs

the wind blew day into night
a dark and turbulent night
accentuating the virgin whiteness
of your skin, unseen by the sun
but not by my eyes
which pierce the night like a sword
to wrap themselves in your image

so i sit looking at your smile
looking until a tear blurs my vision
a vision that holds you
but only on a piece of paper

changes

in walks through fallen leaves
that autumn's brought down
i think of the better times
where carnival rainbows were found

the walks weren't lonely then
two hands were held close there
and the happiness of that moment
now brings me a tear

love notes and paper rings
and things made with cheer
are lost in that memory
of time's changing year

warming touch

morning's echo from the sun
reminds me of your touch
as the light rays of dawn
slowly caress the day
   as you have held my hand
filling the body with energy
   as you have filled my heart with warmth
in days that were just yesterday

my skies are now darkened
for your hand is not there as before
to push away skies of grey
as the sidewalks i walk
are of a concrete cold like my heart
no longer touched by
morning's echo from the sun

a reflection

someone outside tells me i'm lonely
it's only the stars of passing time
telling me man is only
in the shadow of his own mind

sunrise, sunset

the sun shines on for the day
it shines for a long, long time
you came and shone my way

in moments that nourished my mind
but like the sun that has to sleep
your quest will also repeat
the vanishing sun of warmth and light

where memories were, now an emptiness
in the shadow of my mind
where i stand in love's hour of darkness
standing for a long, long time

a flower

love is a rose without thorns
when you first pick it
to hold close in the sun's warmth
but like the seasons that change
so can a flower
when the sun's warmth becomes cold
and love becomes a rose of thorns

shades of autumn

my garden is covered with leaves
silent colours of autumn on the ground
just like tears are these withered leaves
which from my heart have fallen down

my heart stands in a barren loneliness
like the silent emptiness of autumn's trees
soon to be covered by the cold of winter
like my garden which is covered by leaves

white nights

your touch lingers still
in days gone by without you
as thick falls the snow
an incredible silent whiteness
that covers paths that we took
in summer memories
where your touch . . . lingers still

love's shadow

deep blue night of abandoned thoughts
breathing deeply and slowly
the wind calls out my name
weaving echoes in the night
darkness shades the winter
of a tapestry that was once white

the white sands of brightness
go not where i go
for the silence is deep
and colder than the snow

tomorrow, tomorrow
time is so far away
and with it your touch
now gone in yesterday

silent night

touch me night
deep silent night
without stars of brightness
i am without
as i am within
my shadow is lonely here

touch me
as my eyes touch the endless sky
wondering where and who i am
for i have felt the earth and the rain
the wind the sun and the stars
which even now shun their light
the mind of wisdom against me

i have no more familiar signs
symbolic of balance to touch
just clouds of dark fear
that bring me no food or wine
that is felt so deep within
like a burning sensation in the heart
that needs a nourishment to thrive
which is beyond me now
as this lantern dims with the night
eclipsing with it even the fondest
of memories, perhaps they are now withered
like autumn leaves on the ground
falling from a life that thrived
through spring and summer
and nights that turned into day

if only i could wake up and go to sleep
this night which is endless and faceless
as a clock that strikes no time
would perhaps touch me and leave
as she who had shown me
the garden of eden where
the forbidden fruit fell across the path
that she herself had shown me
it laid there, on a lush green grass
endowed in a fragrance that
called out my name and touched
me . . . as did she

the beauty of nature can be
deceptive as can that of a memory
from which i must awaken night
touch me night
deep silent night
without stars of brightness
i am without
as i am within
my shadow is lonely here

touch me